Daniel
The Clash of Cultures

A Study of Daniel 1-6

woodside
BIBLE CHURCH

A Woodside Bible Church Publication

Contributing authors:

C.T. Eldridge, Lauren Frith,
Ryan Russell, Dan Stewart, Tiffani Zale

TABLE OF CONTENTS

A Note from Pastor Chris Brooks

How do you avoid bowing your knee to the idols of your generation? Furthermore, how do you stand strong for God in the face of secular power? To answer these questions, we turn to the Word of God, specifically to the book of Daniel.

Daniel is a book of the Bible that can help those who desire to follow Christ in an increasingly hostile culture. Sound familiar?

In this study, "Daniel: The Clash of Cultures," we'll look at the life of Daniel and his friends as they navigate a culture completely opposite of the Kingdom of God. And we'll learn that, regardless of the battles we may face, God is sovereign over all. The key to surviving the clash of cultures is to trust in God.

As you utilize this resource, I invite you to spend time reading a chapter of Daniel each week and answering the questions in this book that correspond with that chapter of Scripture. Start your times of study with prayer, asking that the Holy Spirit of God will help you understand the spiritual truth you are reading [1 Corinthians 2:9-13].

Then, when you meet in your Life Group, discuss what you read using the "For Group Discussion" section. If you are using this study and are local to metro Detroit, we'd love to connect you to a Life Group. Scan this QR code to get plugged in.

We are excited to begin this journey as a church family, both individually and together, in corporate worship. May God bless us and strengthen our faith and relationships for His glory in this world!

Soli Deo Gloria,

Pastor Chris Brooks
Senior Pastor – Woodside Bible Church

For the Reader

We're so glad you've joined us to study "Daniel: The Clash of Cultures." To help you get the most out of this resource, let's break down the who, what, when, where, and why of Bible study.

WHO?

Bible study is always about God. The reason we read and dig deeper into Scripture is so that we have a better understanding of the Father. When we know God's heart, we can more fully live in His ways and turn away from our own. The book of Daniel highlights the lives of Daniel and his three friends, Shadrach, Meshach, and Abednego. While we will learn a lot about the events of their lives, the focus will always be on what we can understand about God through their experiences and responses to Him.

WHAT?

This resource will help us explore Daniel 1-6. You will first be asked to read each chapter in its entirety, then you will dig deeper using a three-step method of Bible study. When you see these icons, they will indicate what type of question we will be answering about a passage:

Step 1 is to Observe a passage of Scripture. These questions will ask you to look back at the passage and identify information to help you grasp what is happening in the story.

Step 2 is to Understand the passage of Scripture by asking "What does this passage mean?" These questions will help you to interpret the information in the passage for its deeper spiritual meaning.

Step 3 is to Apply what you learn in the passage to your own life. James 1:25 says, "But the one who looks into the perfect law, the law of liberty, and preservers, being no hearer who forgets but a doer who acts, he will be blessed in his doing." These questions will help us to be doers of the Word.

In these **Deep Dive** questions, you will be asked to turn to another part of Scripture that will help you better understand what you are reading in Daniel.

After studying the Bible, it's important to respond to what you are reading through prayer and by identifying steps of obedience. In every chapter, you will see a blank page where you can write out your prayer of response to God. Prompts will be provided for you, and they will follow the ACTS model of prayer:

A is for Adoration: We are called to enter God's presence, praising and loving Him for who He is [Psalm 100:4]. Bible study reveals the truth about God's character that we can rejoice in. And when we see God for who He is, we will praise Him.

C is for Confession: When we see God for the glorious one that He is, we also see ourselves for the sinners that we are. So next, we confess our sin to Him and ask for His forgiveness—which is guaranteed in Christ [1 John 1:9]!

T is for Thanksgiving: Thanking God for His forgiveness naturally flows from confession, but then we move on to remember all He has done for us and how He has answered our prayers.

S is for Supplication: This biblical word simply means making requests. After we have praised God for who He is, confessed our sin, and remembered His works with thanksgiving, we are invited to lay all our cares and concerns before our good Father who hears us and cares for us [1 Peter 5:7, Philippians 4:6-7].

Once you've finished praying, you can use the "respond in obedience" section to write down any practical next steps the Lord has laid on your heart in response to the scripture. Perhaps you need to eliminate something in your life that is coming between you and God. Or maybe, you need to schedule a time to meet with a friend to confess a sin you've been struggling with and seek accountability. There may be a step of active obedience God is asking you to take towards strengthening your relationship with Him.

WHEN?
This resource is intended to be used two separate times each week—once for individual study and once for group discussion.

Individual Study: This section is for you to complete on your own before your Life Group meeting. You can complete the entire section in one sitting or break it up to complete a couple of pages or sections each day of the week. Try it both ways and see which one you like best!

For Group Discussion: This section serves as a discussion guide for your Life Group as your leader guides you through each chapter of Daniel. Most questions are lifted right out of the Individual Study, so if you complete that section beforehand, you will have answers ready to share!

WHERE?
There is something special about studying the Bible in community with others. The first church in Acts 2 "devoted themselves to the apostles' teaching and the fellowship" [v. 42]. Paul's letters were intended to be read aloud and passed among the churches [Colossians 4:16]. Studying Scripture communally unites us together in our faith and helps us to affirm the truth of God's Word.

WHY?
There are many ways to study the Bible and many ways to pray. We have selected just one method of each to repeat as we study Daniel 1-6 [see above under "WHAT?"]. Repetition helps foster patterns of thought and action, which then become habits. By studying and praying the same way each week, we hope to help form your habits of digging deeper into Scripture and responding to God in conversational prayer.

For the Leader
_____

"Daniel: The Clash of Cultures" is a book intended for personal Bible study and small group discussion. Please encourage the members of your Life Group to obtain their own copy and complete the weekly lessons. Doing so will enable them to establish rhythms of time in God's Word each week.

Within each chapter of this book, you will find two sections: an Individual Study section and a For Group Discussion section. The Individual Study section was designed to be completed independently between group meetings, while the For Group Discussion section was designed to help you, as the leader,

facilitate a discussion based on the contents of the chapter. Here's what you'll find in each For Group Discussion section:

Discussion Goal: This section highlights the main ideas in the passage and will help you, as the leader, keep the conversation on track. No need to read this out loud; just keep it in mind as you begin your discussion.

Ice Breaker: Before you dive into the meat of the passage, this question will help your group members open up and get to know one another more. It's intended to be light and fun. Make sure you have everyone share an answer.

Summary: To begin the discussion, you're welcome to have someone read the chapter of Daniel aloud to your group. Alternatively, this summary provides a recap for you to remind everyone of the key events of the narrative in a shorter amount of time, as many of the chapters in Daniel span over thirty verses.

Discussion Questions: These open-ended questions or prompts are meant to spark great conversation amongst your group about the chapter in Daniel. They're organized to follow the passage from top to bottom, addressing each section of the chapter in order. You may notice that most of the questions are repeated from the Individual Study Section, so if your members complete that section ahead of time, they will have answers ready to share during the group discussion.

Life Application: This section was written to prompt your group to identify their next steps for responding to the truth they've learned through the passage. You may be able to agree on a step the entire group can take together. Or you may also find it beneficial to have everyone come up with an individual next step and share it with a friend for accountability. One of the most beautiful things about living in community is the opportunity to point one another towards Christ and hold each other accountable to live a life that is pleasing and honoring to him.

Prayer Requests: Use this section to record your group members' prayer requests during your time together. Don't forget to spend time praying! It's not only a great way to end your group time but also a great way to start it.

Whether you use the For Group Discussion section as a word-for-word script or as a starting point to facilitate a great conversation, we hope you find it helpful. Remember that it's up to you to help your group stay on track during your meetings. The goal of every group discussion should be like the goal of individual study: to observe God's Word, to understand it, and apply it to our lives. However, with group discussion we have the bonus of learning from one another and holding each other accountable.

Context and History of Daniel

The book of Daniel was written in the sixth century by Daniel, one of several young men of noble family exiled from Judah by the conquering Babylonian empire. Babylon had risen to become a world super-power after overthrowing Assyria and Egypt and eventually spreading its reign over the Middle East where it crushed the city of Jerusalem to rubble in 605 BC. Many of the most gifted young men from Jerusalem were carried into Babylon in attempts to assimilate them into the Babylonian culture. As one of the exiles, Daniel experienced this intense immersion and indoctrination of culture, yet he courageously retained his commitment to his God, Yahweh. During his long life in exile, Daniel was used by God as His prophetic mouthpiece to the gentile and Jewish world declaring God's present and future sovereignty and purpose.

The book of Daniel can be divided into two halves. The first half [chapters 1-6] consists of narratives from the life of Daniel and his three friends. Their lives exemplify faithful living in exile and provide noble examples for God's people regarding how to live in a world that is not your home. The second half [chapters 7-12] is prophetic and contains visions of the future, which reassure God's people that He is in control and will be ultimately victorious despite the present opposition and suffering. These two parts are linked beautifully, as the message of the visions in chapters 7-12 reinforce the message of the narratives found in chapters 1-6. This study will focus on the first half of Daniel's book which spans almost the entire 70 years of Judah's exile and captivity.

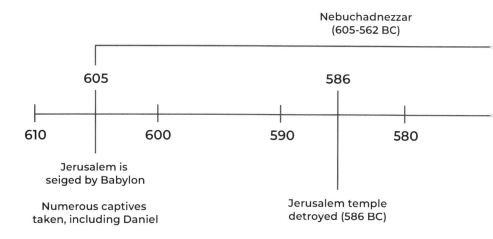

During their time in exile, Daniel and his friends served their pagan masters loyally, settling into life in Babylon as prophets, like Jeremiah [29:5-7], had instructed them to do. Yet even as they lived in this foreign land and culture, they refused to compromise their great allegiance to God. God's powerful sovereign hand gave them wisdom and abilities, such as Daniel's ability to interpret dreams. As a result, Daniel and his friends received favor from their captors, first from King Nebuchadnezzar [605-562 BC] and later King Belshazzar [553-539 BC]. This favor led to them being placed in significant roles of authority over the Babylonian kingdom. Daniel's visions predicted the seemingly untouchable Babylonian empire's eventual fall to Cyrus of the Medo-Persian empire in 539 BC. After this, Daniel was granted ruling authority by Darius [539-530 BC], the Persian governor/king of the realm of the Chaldeans, where he served in faithfully into the rule of Cyrus who eventually allowed the Jews to return home from exile.

The stories in this book are meant to offer hope to God's people who are suffering at the hands of pagan rulers. The readers can find patience as they wait for God's promised deliverance and vindication for His suffering people. The God who directs the forces of history will not abandon his people. They can continue to trust in Him because his promises of redemption and restoration are solidly resting in the coming of the supreme and matchless Messiah.

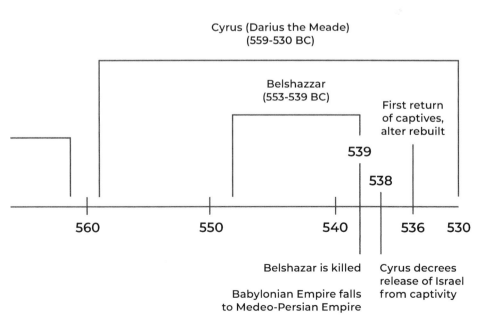

Daniel 1
Faith in a Culture Far from God

"And God gave..." Daniel 1:9a

The worst had happened. The temple had been robbed and desecrated. The best and brightest youth had been taken captive. Babylon—Judah's enemy—came, raided, destroyed, and conquered. The opening verses of Daniel 1 paint a bleak picture indeed.

But those Judeans who knew the scriptures might not have been surprised by this turn of events. When God gave His people the law in Leviticus, He also warned them that if they stopped listening to Him and keeping His commandments, He would allow consequences to befall them—including captivity to their enemies [Leviticus 26:14-17]. And yet, God also promised His people that He would not forget His covenant relationship with those who would be exiled, especially when they responded to His judgments with humility and again turned their hearts back to Him [Leviticus 26:40-45].

Daniel 1 shows us that God is faithful—to both His judgments and His promises. Here, we are introduced to Daniel and his friends. They are among those whose hearts are humble before God, even as they are living in exile in Babylon.

Have you ever felt like life has robbed goodness and joy from you? Where is God in our dark days? When we look at the culture and circumstances around us, it often seems that the enemy is winning. What does Daniel 1 say to us about the character of God and our faithful response amidst difficult circumstances?

Individual Study

Read Daniel 1 in its entirety.

Revisit and focus on Daniel 1:1-7

 OBSERVE

This passage tells us about the activity of the conquering King Nebuchadnezzar. List the things that he took from Judah and what he planned to do with them.

Verse 2 tells us about the activity of God in this event. What does this passage tell us about what God gave?

 UNDERSTAND

King Nebuchadnezzar's goal for Daniel and the other youths from Judah was complete assimilation to the ways of Babylon. What do you think the king's purposes were behind these plans?

 DEEP DIVE

Look up Jeremiah 29:1-14 What does this passage tell us about God's purposes for His people during their exile in Babylon?

 APPLY

How does God's word to His people living in exile in Babylon give you insight into His heart for us, as we live in this world as exiles [1 Peter 2:11-12]? How is your faith being built up through what you have studied here?

Revisit Daniel 1:8-16

 OBSERVE

Did you notice both the repetition and contrast of the phrase "God gave" in verses 2 and 9? What can you learn about God from this?

While Daniel is mentioned in verses 6 and 7, verses 8-16 give us some insight into who he is by his actions. What does Daniel's stand for this faith teach you about him?

 UNDERSTAND

Even though Daniel was living in a foreign culture that did not recognize God, he trusted in God and resolved to keep His commands. What do you think gave Daniel the boldness to stand up for his faith?

 APPLY

What would it look like for you to have that same boldness of faith that Daniel had?

 DEEP DIVE

Read 1 Peter 2:9-12. **Why do you think Peter reminds his readers of their identity in Christ [verses 9-10] before he urges them to live a life that honors God [verses 11-12]?**

Revisit Daniel 1:17-21

 OBSERVE

Verse 17 opens with the third "God gave" of this chapter. What did He give and to whom did He give it?

 UNDERSTAND

Even in the middle of exile, God's favor and blessing remained with His people, Daniel, Hanahiah, Mishael, and Azaria. What does this teach you about God?

 APPLY

How does this story of God's faithfulness in the middle of trial personally encourage you? How have you seen God's favor in your own life?

 DEEP DIVE

Turn to page 6 to review the timeline of Daniel. Notice that Daniel came into Babylon with the first group of exiles and remained there until King Cyrus released the exiles back to Judah [Daniel 1:26]. How does knowing that Daniel remained in God's favor for the duration of the exile [70 years] impact your view of God's faithfulness?

Did you catch this?

It is evident in Daniel 1 that God was in control and working out His purposes as He gave both judgment and favor. Jeremiah 29 gives us insight that the Lord gave favor and blessing to His people in Babylon—specifically to Daniel, Hananiah, Mishael, and Azaria, and the nation and communities to which God allowed them to be exiled. From 2 Chronicles 36, we understand that God was faithful to Daniel through the duration of the exile, even as kings and cultures around him were faithless and sometimes hostile to his God.

Like Daniel and his friends, we each have the gifts and abilities God has determined to give us and are living in the time and place God ordained. Sometimes, our circumstances seem to be out of control, and evil may seem to be winning around us. Remember that we have been shown God's ultimate and eternal favor through the grace given to us in Jesus. Jesus sacrificed His life for us; as a result, the Father has made us His people [1 Peter 2:9-12]. No matter what we face in this world, we live in the favor of God through Christ. And this gives us the power to live obediently, faithfully trusting in Him.

Respond in Prayer

How has this study helped you recognize God's hand in your life? God doesn't always reveal His purposes in our lives, but we can be confident that He is working them out. Use this space to respond in written prayer to what God taught you in Daniel 1. Feel free to use the following prompts to guide your prayers:

- Praise God for what He has shown you about Himself and the way He has revealed His hand in your life.

- Confess the ways that you struggle to believe who God is, and the times when you have not humbled yourself before Him but have chosen instead to do things your own way.

- Thank the Lord that Jesus paid for those sins with His death on the cross so that you can walk guilt-free in God's forgiveness.

- Ask God to help your faith to grow, so that as you trust Him more you will obey Him more.

Prayer

_____

_____

_____

_____

Respond in Obedience

Are there any specific ways that God is asking you to obey Him this week? Write those here and ask the Holy Spirit for power to walk in faithfulness.

_____

_____

_____

For Group Discussion

Discussion Goal: Help your group see how God was both present and in control during Judah's exile and how He blessed Daniel, who trusted in God and remained faithful to Him. Discuss how we, as Christians, can relate to living in exile and what it would look like to trust God and remain faithful to Him in a culture far from Him.

Ice Breaker: Have you ever visited a foreign land or been somewhere you felt out-of-place? Share your experience with the group.

Summary of Daniel 1. Have someone read either Daniel 1 or the summary aloud.

In the opening chapter of Daniel, God gives the king of Judah [who ruled over the nation of God's chosen people, Israel] into the hands of the Babylonian king, Nebuchadnezzar. At that time, several of the brightest and strongest young men in Judah were taken to Babylon [a nation that served other gods] to be trained for service to King Nebuchadnezzar. Among those taken were Daniel, Hanahiah, Mishael, and Azaria.

During training, Daniel resolves to honor God. He boldly requests that he and his friends be allowed to abstain from the king's unclean food and wine. God gives Daniel favor with his supervisor, the chief of eunuchs. The chief hesitates to grant Daniel's request for fear of the king, but trusting in God, Daniel convinces the chief to agree to a ten-day test of this eating arrangement. After ten days, Daniel and his friends are found to be stronger and in better appearance than any of the other trainees. Because of this, the chief allows them to remain faithful in obedience to God.

God gave Daniel, Hanahiah, Mishael, and Azaria skills and wisdom as they trained. He also gave Daniel an understanding of visions and dreams. And after their three-year training period, the King found them to be ten times better in wisdom and understanding than any of those who trained with them or any magicians and enchanters currently serving in the kingdom. Because of this, Daniel remained in royal service until the first year of King Cyrus' reign [the entire duration of the exile].

Discussion Questions

• Daniel 1 opens with God's people being taken into exile, into a foreign land that does not worship God. Paul refers to Christians as exiles in 1 Peter 2:9-12, as heaven is a believer's true home. As a Christian how can you relate to living in a culture that does not honor God? How have you seen the culture we live in influence your life?

• Read Jeremiah 29:4-14. What does this passage tell us about God's plan for His people? How does this passage help us understand what remaining faithful to God looks like in a culture far from Him?

• In Daniel 1:8-16 Daniel makes a bold stand to remain obedient to God. What do you think gave Daniel the boldness to do this? What makes it difficult to stand up for your beliefs? What would it look like for you to have the same boldness Daniel had?

• At the end of Daniel 1, we see how God blessed Daniel, Hanahiah, Mishael, and Azaria in the middle of their exile. How does this story of God's faithfulness encourage you? How have you seen God's favor in your own life?

• Did anything else stand out to you from Daniel 1?

Life Application

It can feel discouraging to be surrounded by a culture that is far from God! Yet, God is faithful! No matter what our circumstances are, He is in control. As a group, discuss how you can remain faithful to God in the middle of your circumstances this week.

_____

_____

_____

_____

_____

Prayer Requests

_____

_____

_____

_____

_____

_____

_____

_____

Notes

Daniel 2

The Greatness of God's Kingdom

"He reveals deep and hidden things; He knows what is in the darkness..."
Daniel 2:22

Have you ever received a gift only for it to be taken away? Chapter one ended with God granting Daniel and his three young friends some incredible gifts: exceptional health, favor with their supervisors, and extraordinary wisdom and understanding. But chapter two records all these gifts being threatened! Nebuchadnezzar, the pagan ruler of Babylon, had a dream and was determined to discover its meaning. When his most advanced wise men failed to reveal it, Nebuchadnezzar gave the order for all his spiritual advisors to be executed, including Daniel and his friends! Their healthy lives could be destroyed, their previous favor now seemed irrelevant, and their wisdom wasn't consulted.

Despite these threats, God demonstrated His sovereign power over the strongest human kings and kingdoms. Any appearance of sovereignty will be dwarfed by God's rule and reign over the affairs of humanity. God's matchless sovereignty provides us with confidence in His promises and empowers us to live our lives in ways that will honor Him.

Daniel 2 shows us that God's kingdom is the greatest. As God provides Daniel with understanding and insight, God's wisdom and power are revealed spectacularly. It is God who ultimately establishes and removes rulers and authorities, and His rule triumphs over them all!

Are there times when you feel threatened by the forces of evil? Do you ever feel anxious that life events may destroy the good things that God has provided? Do you wonder if your efforts to remain true to God's values are futile or pointless? Daniel 2 will provide us with evidence that God is ultimately in control of the events of this world. We will see that our confidence can be rooted in His wisdom and power as He is the God who changes seasons, removes and sets up kings, and gives wisdom and revelation.

Individual Study

Read Daniel 2 in its entirety.

Revisit Daniel 2:1-16

 OBSERVE

King Nebuchadnezzar was upset by a dream he had. What did he demand from the spiritual advisors in his court?

The extent of the king's power and anger is seen in the severity of his response to the inability of his advisors. Why were Daniel and friends in danger because of the "irrational demands" of the king?

 UNDERSTAND

Daniel and his companions were too low in status among the advisors to be brought into the situation until Daniel made his appeal to his supervisor. Not just anyone gained an audience with the king. How do you think Daniel's reputation may have contributed to gaining this audience?

 DEEP DIVE

Look up Deuteronomy 18:10. **The Hebrew people were given clear instructions to stay away from divination, sorcery, etc. And yet, God allowed Daniel and his friends to be "lumped together" with people who were practicing these things. Why do you think He allowed that to happen?**

 APPLY

When we're surrounded by people who do not believe the same things we do, how can God's presence and gift of wisdom empower us to live and speak in such a way that points others to truth?

Revisit Daniel 2:17-30

 OBSERVE

King Nebuchadnezzar was upset by a dream he had. What did he demand from the spiritual advisors in his court?

List some of the characteristics of God that Daniel celebrates in his prayer of thanksgiving to God for revealing the mystery:

 UNDERSTAND

How does Daniel reveal the difference between the power of the spiritual advisors and power of the God of Heaven?

 APPLY

To what situation in your life can you apply the statement, "but there is a God in heaven"?

 DEEP DIVE

Read Colossians 2:1-3. What joy there is for us when we discover that the treasures of wisdom and knowledge are found in Jesus Christ! How does truly knowing Jesus give you wisdom and understanding?

Revisit Daniel 2:31-45

 OBSERVE

In Nebuchadnezzar's dream, what are the four sections of the image?

In Daniel's interpretation, what are the characteristics of each of the four kingdoms?

 UNDERSTAND

1 Peter 2:6-8 connects this image of the stone to Jesus. What are the similarities of this stone in the dream to the person and ministry of Jesus?

 APPLY

How does this story of God's sovereignty over all the powers of humanity personally encourage you? How have you seen God's powerful rule in your own life?

 DEEP DIVE

Turn to page 6 to review the timeline of Daniel.
The dream would have been given early in Nebuchadnezzar's reign.
There would be several decades before these kingdom changes would
take place. How would this revelation provide Daniel with confidence
despite the lengthy exile in Babylon? How does Christ's coming Kingdom
provide you with confidence?

Revisit Daniel 2:46-49

 OBSERVE

What opinion of God does Nebuchadnezzar form because of
this experience?

 UNDERSTAND

Daniel requested that his three companions also be given roles of
authority in the provinces of Babylon. How does this promotion of God's
people to higher levels of authority demonstrate that God's rule is greater
than kingdoms of this world?

 APPLY

What are some of the atrocities in our present time that can tempt us to wonder if God is truly in control?

Did you catch this?

Many people who read about this fantastic dream tend to spend most of their time considering its meaning, which is certainly fascinating. However, the main point of the story is not the dream itself but rather to show the superiority of the Lord's wisdom above the wisdom of the Babylonians. True wisdom comes from the God of Heaven, who gives it to those who worship Him. Daniel and his friends were recognized as superior in health, skill, and understanding. Their mastery of the Babylonian training process was thought to have given them superiority of mind. But in this chapter, we learn that this wisdom [magic, sorcery, and philosophy] leads the advisors nowhere.

Daniel and his prayer partners demonstrated the type of wisdom described throughout the Scriptures, which declares that the "fear of the LORD is the beginning of wisdom" [Proverbs 1:7]. As they depended on the Lord and turned to Him in prayer, they received the revelation that was needed. This story affirms that true wisdom comes only from Him and is freely given to His children who love and honor Him.

Respond in Prayer

How has this study helped you recognize God's rule over all the affairs of humanity? Sometimes, we feel that circumstances can threaten His blessings in our lives, but Christ's victory assures us that our God can be trusted. Use this space to respond in written prayer to what God taught you in Daniel 2. Feel free to use the following prompts to guide your prayers:

• Praise God for what He has shown you about Himself and the way He rules in our world.

• Confess the times that you doubt His authority and involvement in the challenges that you face.

• Thank the Lord for His forgiveness in your times of doubt and unbelief in His sovereign hand.

• Ask God to give you heavenly wisdom and understanding as you live for Him in times of challenge and opposition.

_____

_____

_____

_____

_____

Respond in Obedience

Are there any specific ways that God is asking you to obey Him this week? Write those here and ask the Holy Spirit for power to walk in faithfulness.

_____

_____

_____

_____

_____

For Group Discussion

Discussion Goal: Help your group view present circumstances and challenges through the lens of God's supremacy. No kingdom is greater than His, and He provides wisdom and change so that He is made known throughout all the world. Discuss how we can live with humble confidence that God will be exalted over everything and that we are also victors in Christ.

Ice Breaker: When's the last time you took on a task that was outside of your personal expertise? Share how it went with the group.

Summary of Daniel 2. Have someone read either Daniel 2 or the summary aloud.

Early in Nebuchadnezzar's reign, he had a dream that greatly disturbed him. He demanded that his leading spiritual advisors not only tell him the dream's meaning but also reveal the dream itself. To ensure that these "magicians, enchanters, and sorcerers" were trustworthy in their responses.

When they exclaimed that no man could do such a thing, the king furiously demanded the execution of all the wise men in the kingdom. This group of condemned advisors included Daniel, Hananiah, Mishael, and Azariah. These men, whom God provided supernatural provision and favor during their Babylonian training, were now facing the same death sentence as the pagan advisors. In response, Daniel asked the king for time to seek the revelation of the dream.

Daniel and his friends prayed and sought God's wisdom. God graciously revealed to Daniel both the dream and the interpretation. After Daniel responded to God's provision with a beautiful prayer of worship, he brought the revelation to the king. He credited the God of Heaven for making known the dream and the message that would reveal the destiny of future kingdoms of the world.

The dream centered around an imposing statue with a head of gold, a torso of silver, a midsection of bronze, legs of iron, and feet of a mixture of iron and clay. A large stone struck the statue, crushed every section, and became a massive mountain. Daniel revealed that the dream disclosed the present kingdom and those that would come after it. God's kingdom would break apart all earthly kingdoms and remain the only kingdom to stand forever.

Knowing that the revelation was true, Nebuchadnezzar humbly acknowledged God as the greatest of all gods and revealer of mysteries. He promoted Daniel and his friends as rulers in his realm, with Daniel as leader over all the king's advisors.

Discussion Questions

- The king's demand on his advisors was humanly impossible to fulfill, and the death sentence appeared certain. Yet, Daniel and his friends knew their God could do the impossible. How does their faith inspire you? What impossible situation in your own life can you apply the statement, "But there is a God in heaven?"

- Daniel 2 reveals that true wisdom comes from God alone. Read James 1:5-8 out loud. How does knowing you can ask God for wisdom impact you? Even when we're surrounded by people who do not believe the same things we do, how can God's presence and gift of wisdom empower us to live and speak in such a way that points others to the truth?

- In Daniel's prayer of worship [2:20-23], Daniel acknowledged God as the one who gives wisdom, changes situations, and establishes positions of power. What situations in our world or in your life does God bring to your mind that need to be viewed from this reality? What are some of the atrocities in our present time that can tempt us to wonder if God is truly in control?

- The revelation of the dream provided Nebuchadnezzar with the recognition that there is no God like Yahweh. What has God revealed about Himself to you through the ways He has worked in your life?

- How will your life be affected this week by what you have observed in Daniel 2?

Life Application

Circumstances in our world can feel daunting and seem as if God is not truly reigning over it all. Knowing that He gives understanding to those who seek Him, changes situations that seem unchangeable, and places and removes authorities that appear untouchable provides us with a confidence and security that nothing else can. As a group, discuss the way your outlook can change when you view things through the lens of God's supremacy.

Prayer Requests

Notes

Daniel 3
Faith in the Furnace

"Our God whom we serve is able to deliver us from the burning fiery furnace, and he will deliver us....But if not,...we will not serve your gods or worship the golden image...." Daniel 3:17-18

King Nebuchadnezzar was not to be trifled with. Like powerful dictators of more recent times, he ruled through fear and kept order with violence.

In Daniel 2, we saw that God had a message for King Nebuchadnezzar about the future of his empire—that it would eventually crumble like a statue with clay feet. But it seems that the king wanted to prove that prediction wrong because Daniel 3 opens with a description of a 90-foot high by nine-foot-wide solid gold statue that Nebuchadnezzar had made. You can almost hear the king saying to himself and God, "I'll show you how powerful I am!"

Strangely enough, the plain of Dura on which King Nebuchadnezzar built this golden image was the same plain on which the Tower of Babel was started in Genesis 11:2 [The story in Genesis 11:1-9 is a quick read if you aren't familiar with it]. These two accounts are strikingly similar—not only because of the tall objects being built on the same plain but also because of the hidden motives of the human heart being revealed. They shine a light on the desires of all cultures of the world in all of history: People want to be worshipped rather than worship their Creator. Leaders want to unify the world as proof of their own greatness rather than pointing to the greatness of God. Everyone wants to follow the ways that seem right in their own eyes rather than submit to the ways of the Lord.

As followers of Jesus, we know the end of the story—that Jesus will ultimately be the ruler of all the nations and worshipped by all people. But how are we supposed to remain faithful and obedient to God now when the culture around us encourages the opposite? Like Nebuchadnezzar in Babylon, people in our world make much of themselves in opposition to God. And sometimes, they are openly hostile to God and His ways. Where can we find strength to stand for what God says is right, even amid difficult circumstances?

Individual Study

Read Daniel 3 in its entirety.

Revisit Daniel 3:1-15

 OBSERVE

Count the number of times Daniel tells us that King Nebuchadnezzar "made" or "set up" the golden image. What do you think he may be trying to communicate about the nature of this idol?

And what does King Nebuchadnezzar's question at the end of v. 15 reveal about his heart?

 DEEP DIVE

Look up Exodus 20:3. What is the first of God's commandments to His people, Israel?

UNDERSTAND

King Nebuchadnezzar ruled a totalitarian state through violence and fear. In response to the king's edict, only three men were found still standing, choosing not to bow down to the golden idol [v. 12]. Shadrach, Meshach, and Abednego discerned that this was an issue of obedience to the first of the Ten Commandments. In what ways might they have justified bowing down to the image in that cultural moment?

APPLY

What is one way that you have had to stand apart from cultural influences—whether in action or in attitude—to worship God through your obedience?

If you can't think of a way, pray, and ask the Lord to help you discern any heart attitudes that may be directed by the values of the world rather than by the worship of God. Making choices to hold God highest in our hearts will help us practice obedience in small and big ways.

Revisit Daniel 3:16-18

 OBSERVE

What did Shadrach, Meshach, and Abednego know for sure?

What were they not sure of?

 UNDERSTAND

These three men had courageous faith in the face of an evil and hostile king, even when they weren't sure what God was going to do for them. How do you think God's past actions in their lives [see 1:11-17 and 2:17-19] shaped their confidence in his faithfulness, character, and ability?

 APPLY

What is one area of your life that feels uncertain right now? What aspects of God's character give you faith to obey Him even when you don't know how He may work in this situation?

Revisit Daniel 3:19-30

 OBSERVE

List the ways God showed His power in these verses.

 DEEP DIVE

Read Isaiah 43:1-2. **God never promises to keep us out of life's fires or deep waters. What DOES He promise in this passage?**

 UNDERSTAND

Interpretations vary about who the "fourth man" in the fire might have been. Some say it was an angel sent by God [see v. 28]. However, it was probably God Himself in the form of the pre-incarnate Christ [see Nebuchadnezzar's reference "the fourth is like a son of the gods" in v. 25]. How does this help us to apply and take comfort in what Isaiah 43:1-2 says?

 DEEP DIVE

Turn to Romans 8:31-37. While God spared Shadrach, Meshach, and Abednego from the fire, He did not spare His own Son from death on the cross. Even worse, Jesus faced His personal fiery furnace experience alone and forsaken by God [see Matthew 27:46]. Because Jesus walked through the fire for us and experienced God's ultimate deliverance through resurrection from the dead, what promises can God now make to us through Christ, recorded here in Romans?

 APPLY

What fire are you currently walking through? Which promises from Isaiah and Romans will help you turn to God in the hard times rather than put your trust in anyone or anything else?

Did you catch this?

Courageous faith in the face of hostility and trials is built on obedience to God's Word in response to His faithfulness. Shadrach, Meshach, and Abednego obeyed the 1st Commandment [Exodus 20:3] to worship no other gods—even if it meant facing death. Their experiences of God's power and faithfulness in Daniel 1 and 2 must have given them confidence that God is the one true God and is more powerful and worthy of worship than anyone else.

While we can never be sure how God will choose to act in any given situation, we can be sure of our ultimate deliverance through the death and resurrection of Jesus [Romans 8:31-37]. God doesn't promise to keep us out of fires, danger, or distress, but He does promise to walk with us through it all [Isaiah 43:1-2]. We know that God will never leave us because Jesus died for us. He was forsaken by God, so we don't have to be. When we put our faith in Jesus, we can trust that God will always be with us. Praise be to God!

Respond in Prayer

What fires are you walking through right now? God's promised presence in our trials is a rock we can cling to in uncertain times. Use this space to respond in written prayer to what God taught you in Daniel 3. Feel free to use the following prompts as a guide:

• Praise God for His record of faithfulness—walking through fire with Shadrach, Meshach, and Abednego and being true to His promises through trials in your own life [Romans 8:31-37].

• Confess the ways that you are tempted to compromise your obedience to God in a culture that leads us to believe that following Him is not worth it.

• Thank the Lord that Jesus experienced separation from God in death so that you would never have to. And thank Him for the ways you have felt His presence this week.

• Tell God about the feelings and fears you are experiencing in the fires and deep waters you are facing right now. Ask God to show you how to stay strong in obedience as you cling to His promises.

_____

_____

_____

_____

_____

_____

_____

Respond in Obedience

Are there any specific ways that God is asking you to obey Him this week? Write those here and ask the Holy Spirit for the power to walk in faithfulness.

_____

_____

_____

_____

_____

_____

_____

For Group Discussion

Discussion Goal: Help group members understand that following God may require us to stand courageously against cultural influences. However, remind them that God's promises to walk with us through difficult circumstances are what allow us to remain faithful to Him. Help the group make the connection that Jesus walked through the fire of death for us so that when we trust Him with our lives and for salvation, He now walks with us in our fiery furnaces of life.

Ice Breaker: Describe the hottest place you have ever been. Where was it and what was it like?

Summary of Daniel 3. Have someone read either Daniel 3 or the summary aloud.

King Nebuchadnezzar set up a golden image, 90-feet-high and nine-feet wide, in the plain of Dura in Babylon. Then, he invited all government officials from his empire's provinces to attend a dedication ceremony. He commanded all the people to fall down and worship the golden image when the sound of the music began, threatening that anyone who wouldn't be thrown into a fiery furnace. So, all the people did what the king commanded...except for Shadrach, Meshach, and Abednego, Daniel's three friends from Judah, who had been appointed to government positions in Babylon.

Certain jealous officials told the king that Shadrach, Meshach, and Abednego paid no attention to his command. King Nebuchadnezzar was furious and brought the three men before him. He repeated his edict, instructing them to fall down at the sound of the music and worship the golden image he made, promising that he would cast them into a burning fiery furnace if they disobeyed. Shadrach, Meshach, and Abednego replied with faith that God would be able to deliver them from the burning fiery furnace and out of the king's hand, and even if He [God] didn't, they would still never serve the king's gods or worship his golden image.

King Nebuchadnezzar was enraged and ordered the furnace to be heated seven times hotter. He had Shadrach, Meshach, and Abednego bound up and thrown into the furnace by mighty men from his army. The fire was so hot that these men were killed when they came close to the flames, but very quickly, the king was astonished to see that Shadrach, Meshach, and Abednego were walking in the furnace, unbound and unhurt. He also noted that there was a fourth man in the furnace with them who had the appearance of "a son of the gods" [v. 25]. He called Shadrach, Meshach, and Abednego out of the furnace and, along with all his government officials, saw that the men were unharmed by the fire—not a hair was singed, their clothes were not burned, and there was not even the smell of smoke on them.

The king blessed God, who had protected His servants in the fire. And he recognized the surrendered faith of Shadrach, Meshach, and Abednego. He issued a new decree that anyone in his kingdom who spoke against the God of these men would be punished, acknowledging that there was no other god who could make this rescue. Finally, he promoted Shadrach, Meshach, and Abednego as officials in Babylon.

Discussion Questions

• Shadrach, Meshach, and Abednego were the only three in the empire who stood against the king's order to worship his golden image. What is one way that you have had to stand apart from cultural influences— whether in action or in attitude—to worship God through your obedience? Or how do you think God might be preparing you to do so?

• God never promises that we won't go through hard times; on the contrary, He says that when we do, He will be with us [read Isaiah 43:1-2 aloud together now]. Shadrach, Meshach, and Abednego had confidence in God's capabilities and character, partly because they had already seen Him work in their lives.

• What is one area of your life that feels uncertain right now? What aspects of God's character give you faith to obey Him even when you don't know how He may work in this situation?

• Read Romans 8:31-37 aloud. Because Jesus walked through the fire for us, and experienced God's ultimate deliverance through resurrection from the dead, what promises can God now make to us through Christ, recorded here in Romans?

• What fire are you currently walking through? Which promises from Isaiah and Romans will help you turn to God in the hard times rather than put your trust in anyone or anything else?

• Did anything else stand out to you from Daniel 3?

Life Application

God's faithfulness prompts courageous faith in us. As a group discuss what next steps you need to take to in response to this week's lesson.

_____

_____

_____

_____

_____

Prayer Requests

_____

_____

_____

_____

_____

_____

_____

_____

_____

Notes

Daniel 4

Heaven Rules

"...the Most High rules the kingdom of men and gives it to whom he will and sets over it the lowliest of men." Daniel 4:17b

---

During his reign, King Nebuchadnezzar was arguably the most powerful person on the planet. Monuments were erected in his honor, buildings were built with his name on them, and his kingdom was as vast as the world had ever known. Nebuchadnezzar isn't necessarily wrong when he rhetorically asks in 4:30, "Is not this great Babylon, which I have built by my mighty power as a royal residence and for the glory of my majesty?" There was a greatness, a power, and a majesty to his kingdom that outmatched every other earthly kingdom that had come before.

However, Nebuchadnezzar's accomplishments and power went to his head. He forgot that he was a mere man. Notice in that same verse from above that he says, "Is not this great Babylon, which I have built by my mighty power..." Statements like this one are an offense to God. Nebuchadnezzar was so impressed with himself that he had no room for God in his life. This shouldn't surprise us after reading about Nebuchadnezzar's pride and arrogance in chapters two and three.

However, Daniel 4 ultimately highlights the mercy of God. Yes, we see God's justice walking Nebuchadnezzar through this season of humiliation, but this humbling process ultimately leads Nebuchadnezzar to mercifully realize that "the Most High rules the kingdom of men and gives it to whom he will" (4:17b, 25b, 32b).

Have you ever been so impressed with yourself that you lost focus on God? What events in your life have served to remind you of your humble place before God. Let's meditate on the testimony of King Nebuchadnezzar and behold the power of God to humble those who walk in pride (4:37).

Individual Study

Read Daniel 4 in its entirety.

Revisit Daniel 4:1-27

 OBSERVE

These verses tell us about King Nebuchadnezzar's second dream. In your own words, briefly describe some of the details of his dream.

At the end of his interpretation of King Nebuchadnezzar's dream, Daniel tells the king how he should respond. What does Daniel tell him to do?

 UNDERSTAND

Verse 4 tells us that Nebuchadnezzar "was at ease in [his] house and prospering in [his] palace" when this dream interrupts things for him. Why do you think this specific piece of context would be given just before the dream and its interpretation are described?

 APPLY

God doesn't allow Nebuchadnezzar to float through life and enjoy the cozy experience of being king. Instead, He interrupts things with this dream that tells Nebuchadnezzar the truth about Himself. How has God interrupted your life with His truth before? How is He speaking to you now and confronting your sin as He did Nebuchadnezzar?

 DEEP DIVE

Read Mark 10:42-45. Contrast Jesus' teaching on leadership with Nebuchadnezzar's mindset. How does Jesus as the Son of Man and King of kings show us what true leadership and greatness look like?

Revisit Daniel 4:28-33

OBSERVE

Did you notice the repetition of the phrase "the Most High rules the kingdom of men and gives it to whom he will" [vv. 17, 25, 32]? What differences are there between the way this sentence is stated in these three different verses?

What are some of the effects on Nebuchadnezzar after he experiences God's judgment?

UNDERSTAND

After Nebuchadnezzar experiences God's judgment, he becomes like an animal. What do you think is the significance of Nebuchadnezzar going through such a transformation?

 APPLY

**When has God humbled [even humiliated] you because of your arrogance?
How did this experience help you grow in humility?**

 DEEP DIVE

Read Proverbs 16:18. **What is it about pride and having a "haughty spirit"
that leads us to destruction? How does the good news of Jesus counteract
this pride?**

Revisit Daniel 4:34-37

 OBSERVE

**After Nebuchadnezzar's "reason returned" to him, what else then
returned to him?**

What about God's kingdom and dominion are emphasized in these verses?

UNDERSTAND

The Bible teaches that all people have value and worth [Genesis 1:27], but Daniel 4:35 says that "all the inhabitants of the earth are accounted as nothing." Considering the surrounding context, what does this phrase in v. 35 mean?

APPLY

Like Nebuchadnezzar, how have you seen God's grace restore you from disgraceful situations?

DEEP DIVE

Read Ephesians 2:1-10. What gospel truths speak to the restorative power of God? In other words, how does Jesus take us from the depths of depravity to the glories of our heavenly status?

Did you catch this?

Daniel 4 is a clear warning, not only to kings and people in authority but to all of us. Arrogance is lethal. Thinking of ourselves more highly than we ought leads to division in the church, bitterness between friends, and apathy in worship [Romans 12:3]. In Proverbs 16:18, King Solomon tells us that "Pride goes before destruction," and he wasn't kidding. The humiliating process that God led Nebuchadnezzar through was painful and embarrassing. Nebuchadnezzar experienced God's judgment for his "haughty spirit" [Proverbs 16:18] and arrogant attitude.

But in the Gospels, we hear good news about a different kind of king. In Mark 10:45, Jesus describes Himself as the Son of Man. This title is of the utmost relevance when it comes to the book of Daniel. In Daniel 7, the prophet receives a vision of "one like a son of man" who ascends to heaven and receives the eternal kingdom of God [7:13-14]. Despite Nebuchadnezzar's greatness, he could never come close to the majesty and glory of King Jesus. And yet, Jesus shows us that true kingship and leadership are not found in building monuments, piling our accomplishments, or proving our genius. A true king lays aside his rights and privileges as a king to serve, just as Jesus did for us on the cross.

Respond in Prayer

How has this study helped illuminate the arrogance in your heart? Our pride isn't always easy to see, but the Spirit illuminates our hearts and shows us our sin. Use this space to respond in written prayer to what God taught you in Daniel 4. Use the following prompts to guide your prayers:

- Glorify God for what He has taught you about His character and His Son, the true King.

- Share honestly with God about times when you have thought more highly of yourself than you ought.

- Express gratitude to God for the grace of King Jesus that covers your failures and renews your spirit.

• Seek God for His Spirit to teach you true humility and to help you cultivate servant-heartedness.

_____

_____

_____

_____

_____

_____

_____

Respond in Obedience

Are there any specific ways that God is asking you to obey Him this week? Write those here and ask the Holy Spirit for power to walk in faithfulness.

_____

_____

_____

_____

_____

_____

_____

For Group Discussion

Discussion Goal: Help your group understand that "the Most High rules the kingdom of men and gives it to whom he will and sets over it the lowliest of men" [4:17b]. Like Nebuchadnezzar, if we think that we build our own kingdoms, then we will fall into the trap of arrogance and pride.

Ice Breaker: Who would you say is currently the most powerful person in the world and why?

Summary of Daniel 4. Have someone read either Daniel 4 or the summary aloud.

Daniel 4 begins and ends with King Nebuchadnezzar praising God because "those who walk in pride he is able to humble" [4:37]. The middle sections of the chapter give Nebuchadnezzar's testimony of how God humbled him.

The king's story of learning humility starts with yet another dream. This time, Nebuchadnezzar dreams about a large and beautiful tree. The height of the tree reaches the heavens, and the tree can be seen from the ends of the earth. The branches of the tree are strong and provide housing for birds. Its branches also bear fruit and feed many people. However, a heavenly being [called a "watcher"] descends from heaven and pronounces that the tree is to be destroyed. The only thing left is the stump, which is bound in bands of iron and bronze. The watcher then begins to describe the stump as if it's a person. He says that the stump will change its mind from a man to a beast, and it will live amongst the beasts of the field for seven periods of time.

Daniel then interprets that the dream is Nebuchadnezzar and his kingdom. The tree is Nebuchadnezzar's kingdom, and the stump is Nebuchadnezzar himself. Nebuchadnezzar's kingdom will be taken from him, and he will then lose his mind and live among the beasts.

Despite receiving the warning of this dream, Nebuchadnezzar does not immediately repent of his pride, but he goes on living in arrogance and gloating about his accomplishments as king. Then, a voice from heaven says to the king that his kingdom and sanity will be taken from him. Nebuchadnezzar loses his mind and lives among the beasts of the field as an animal.

But God, in His mercy, eventually leads Nebuchadnezzar to come back to his senses and repent of his pride. God then restores Nebuchadnezzar's kingdom to him, as Nebuchadnezzar closes the chapter by worshipping and praising God because "those who walk in pride he is able to humble" [4:37].

Discussion Questions

• God interrupts Nebuchadnezzar's cozy, kingly life with a disruptive dream that sheds light on the truth about himself. How has God interrupted your life with His truth before? Share how it impacted your life with the group.

• Nebuchadnezzar fell into the trap of pride because of his earthly accomplishments and power, but God humbled him in a major way. What circumstances have led you to grow in pride and arrogance? How have you [like Nebuchadnezzar] been humbled by God after an experience of pride?

• In His grace and mercy, God restored Nebuchadnezzar [v.34-37]. How have you seen God's grace restore you from disgraceful situations?

• Reread Ephesians 2:4-10. What truth stands out to you from this passage and why? How does Jesus take us from the depths of depravity to the glories of our heavenly status, even when it seems like we're too far gone?

• What are ways that you can cultivate humility in your life? How might weekly, corporate worship be an opportunity to nurture humility in your heart?

Life Application

It can be easy to become impressed with ourselves and confident in our abilities. But God is faithful and merciful to help us live lives of lowliness and service before Him. As a group discuss, one way that you can demonstrate Christ-like, humble service to those around you.

_____

_____

_____

_____

_____

Prayer Requests

_____

_____

_____

_____

_____

_____

_____

Notes

Daniel 5
The Writing is [Literally] on the Wall...

"And you his son, Belshazzar, have not humbled your heart, though you knew all this..." Daniel 5:22

The night we're looking at is October 12, 539 B.C. We don't know exactly how much time has passed between the end of Daniel 4 and the beginning of Daniel 5, but we know these stories in Daniel's life are put together for a very intentional purpose. In Daniel 4, King Nebuchadnezzar makes an astounding proclamation, extolling and honoring the "King of heaven." This happens after a supernaturally humbling event in his life.

Enter King Belshazzar. Who likely isn't actually the king but is a spoiled and privileged character who is the crown prince of the current king, Nabonidus. We're looking at the final night of King Belshazzar's life, who also experiences a supernaturally humbling event. However, his response is very different than King Nebuchadnezzar's, and he will reap the consequences.

These two stories are put together to reveal God's sovereign authority over ungodly kings and kingdoms and teach the reader that supernatural revelation ought to lead to humility of heart, leading to the praise and honor of the one true God. The Babylonians had other gods who were believed to have the power to predict the future, but there is only one God who truly has that power and authority. As you study and read, pay attention to what God is doing through the exchange between King Belshazzar and Daniel. This type of interchange is meant to reveal to us the disastrous consequences of rejecting God's reign.

Individual Study

Read Daniel 5 in its entirety.

Revisit Daniel 5:1-12

 OBSERVE

Record details from these verses that give evidence of King Belshazzar's pride and arrogance.

How does his attitude change after seeing the hand writing on the wall?

 UNDERSTAND

How does Daniel's later interpretation [verses 22-23] help us understand that Belshazzar was doing more than just looking for new tableware when he used the vessels from the temple in Jerusalem to serve his guests? What was really going on in Belshazzar's heart?

 APPLY

In this passage, we see the king's pride begin to fall when he is confronted by fear. The only thing that seemed to shake him into self-awareness was the hand God sent to write on the wall during this feast.   When has a hard or shocking situation been the "hand writing on the wall" for you—a situation God used to arrest your attention and cause you to see the sinful state of your heart? Is there anything He is using to help you reevaluate your life, choices, or the state of your heart?

 DEEP DIVE

Look up Deuteronomy 29:29. According to this verse, God doesn't always reveal His thoughts or His ways to us. But when He does, through His Word or through our circumstances, what does He want us to do?

Revisit Daniel 5:13-23

 OBSERVE

In Daniel's speech to the king, what pattern of sin from the days of Nebuchadnezzar does Daniel connect to King Belshazzar?

How had King Belshazzar chosen to respond to the Most High God in his life, despite knowing King Nebuchadnezzar's history? [See verses 21b-22]

 UNDERSTAND

Having the right information about God doesn't guarantee someone's heart will change. In what way does Belshazzar prove this conclusion? In what ways have you experienced this to be true?

 DEEP DIVE

Look up Ezekiel 36:26-27. What does God reveal to His people through the prophet Ezekiel about how true heart change happens?

APPLY

Through the insight He gave Daniel, God offered Belshazzar the opportunity to see the patterns of sin that were being repeated in his life. What patterns of sin might God be revealing in your life? And how has your heart responded to this revelation? How might Ezekiel 36:26-27 change the way you pray about these sin patterns?

Revisit Daniel 5:24-31

OBSERVE

What was the interpretation of the writing on the wall?

UNDERSTAND

God is the "Judge of all the earth [and will] do what is just" [Genesis 18:25c], and the "wages of sin is death" [Romans 6:23]. How does this message to Belshazzar confirm God's rightful place as judge over all?

DEEP DIVE

It seems strange that this message, written in a language that should've been familiar to most who read it, wasn't able to be understood, doesn't it? *Look up 2 Corinthians 4:4-6.* What do these verses reveal about why some people can understand God's revelation and some cannot?

What phrases in these verses reiterate that our understanding of God's message comes through the person of Jesus?

APPLY

Praise God that the "wages of sin is death, but the free gift of God is eternal life in Christ Jesus our Lord" [Romans 6:23]. Jesus takes our judgement that we deserve for our sin and gives us eternal life instead!

In what ways have you experienced freedom from God's judgement? And how have you experienced the light of God's knowledge shining in your heart through Jesus?

Did you catch this?

King Belshazzar knew the story of King Nebuchadnezzar. Still, instead of recognizing and humbling himself before the Most High God, he blatantly disregarded and blasphemed God, using articles from the temple in Jerusalem to serve wine to the guests at his feast. When God supernaturally interrupted the feast, Belshazzar could not understand God's message to him, as is true of all whose minds are darkened by sin and Satan [2 Corinthians 4:4].

This story makes clear that information alone does not cause someone to have a change of heart toward God. We often see patterns of sin repeated from one generation to another, as we see with the pride of Nebuchadnezzar and Belshazzar. The difference in their responses to God's interruption in their lives—Nebuchadnezzar's humility toward God in Daniel 4 and Belshazzar's rejection of God in Daniel 5—determined the end of each of their stories. God is the righteous and rightful judge over His creation. His purposes will stand, and He has the final word over those who reject Him, even powerful rulers and kingdoms.

But He is also a God who wants to communicate with us! He wants us to understand and obey what He reveals to us [Deuteronomy 29:29]. Thanks be to God that, through the light of Jesus in our hearts, He helps us understand His gospel of good news [2 Corinthians 4:6]. He poured out the judgment that we deserve onto His son, Jesus, who died in our place. And then, He placed His Spirit in our hearts to make it possible to live in obedience to Him [Ezekiel 36:26-27]. When we submit to God's rule rather than reject it, there is grace and understanding in God's word to us.

Respond in Prayer

How has this study helped you recognize God's sovereignty and His desire to communicate with us? With chapters four and five mirroring one another in a sense, what have you learned about God's character? Use this space to respond in written prayer to what God taught you in Daniel 5. Feel free to use the following prompts to guide your prayers:

• Adore God for the ways He has shown you Himself through His "handwritten" messaging in your life and through Jesus.

• Confess to God where you might be "missing the message," choosing not to repent of known sin, blasphemy, or idolatry in your life.

• Thank God that Jesus paid for those sins with His death on the cross so that you can walk guilt-free in God's forgiveness.

• With supplication [humble, submissive asking], ask God to help you understand His messages in your life through the light that Christ shines in our hearts so you can walk in obedience with Him more faithfully through the power of his Spirit.

_____

_____

_____

_____

_____

Respond in Obedience

Are there any specific ways that God is asking you to obey Him this week? Write those here and ask the Holy Spirit for power to walk in faithfulness.

_____

_____

_____

_____

_____

For Group Discussion

Discussion Goal: Help your group see God's sovereignty over kings and kingdoms, and His desire to communicate truth about Himself with His creation. Everyone should think through times when "the writing has been on the wall" in their lives; as a group, discuss how God has met you in those times.

Ice Breaker: Share about a time when you or someone else clearly "missed the message." Did something funny or disastrous happen as a result?

Summary of Daniel 5. Have someone read either Daniel 5 or the summary aloud.

Daniel 5 opens with the scene of a huge party that gets supernaturally crashed. This party revealed that King Belshazzar's heart had rejected the Most High God and His rightful reign. He blasphemed God by using items from the temple in Jerusalem to serve wine to his guests. God "crashed" King Belshazzar's party by writing out a message on the wall through a disembodied hand. No one could decipher the mysterious message—none of the enchanters, astrologers, or wise men that Belshazzar assembled—until the queen mother remembered Daniel.

Daniel was summoned. Before addressing the message on the wall, he reminded Belshazzar of the story of Nebuchadnezzar's humbling before God [from Daniel 4] and, by contrast, identified the king's arrogant heart before God. Daniel then correctly read and interpreted the handwriting on the wall, which declared God's judgment on the king and the impending division of his kingdom. That very night, God's judgment came to pass when the Medes and the Persians invaded, killing Belshazzar and conquering the kingdom of Babylon.

Discussion Questions

• In the opening party scene of Daniel 5, we see King Belshazzar's pride and arrogance on display. But God disrupts the party [and Belshazzar's life] with a jarring event! Have you experienced a hard or shocking situation that became the "handwriting on the wall" for you—a situation that caused you to see the sinful state of your heart? Share about that time with the group. What was the situation, and how did it affect you?

• When Daniel interprets the writing on the wall [v. 17-23], he reminds Belshazzar of all God did in the life of King Nebuchadnezzar, information Belshazzar surely would've already known. Having the right information about God doesn't guarantee someone's heart will change. In what ways have you experienced this to be true in your life or the lives of others?

• Read Ezekiel 36:26-27. What does God reveal to His people through the prophet Ezekiel about how true heart change happens? Share a time when your heart was hard, but God gave you a "heart of flesh" towards Himself, another person, or a situation.

• The writing on the wall meant harsh judgment for King Belshazzar, death, and the fall of his kingdom [v.24-31]. As believers, Jesus has saved us from experiencing what Belshazzar experienced [Romans 6:23]. In what ways have you experienced freedom from God's judgment? And how have you experienced the light of God's knowledge shining in your heart through Jesus [2 Corinthians 4:6]?

• Did anything else stand out to you from Daniel 5?

Life Application

God always sees and knows everything. He's also always offering the opportunity to look to Jesus Christ for forgiveness of sin. He's been so kind to deliver personal messages to each of us, calling us to repent. Pray for courage as a group, then discuss how you can honor God by letting go of pride and embracing humility in thought, word, and deed.

_____

_____

_____

_____

_____

Prayer Requests

_____

_____

_____

_____

_____

_____

_____

_____

Notes

Daniel 6
Faith in the Face of Lions

"So Daniel was taken up out of the den, and no kind of harm was found on him, because he had trusted in his God" Daniel 6:23b

---

As we open on Daniel chapter 6, we see the prophetic message Daniel interpreted in chapter five [v. 25-28] continuing to be fulfilled. King Belshazzar has been killed, and Darius the Mede has come into power. As the new king, Darius divided the kingdom into several provinces, placing various leaders, or satraps, over it all. Daniel, who was put into the position of third ruler over the kingdom by Belshazzar, remains a high official. He distinguishes himself as such an excellent leader that King Darius plans to promote him to rule over the entire kingdom.

This final familiar story of Daniel in the lion's den takes place over 60 years after the events we read about in chapter one. Daniel has now lived in exile under the reign of several foreign and wicked kings. Everything around him has changed, but the opening events mentioned above, and the events that will follow, highlight some of the most important things that have remained the same: God's control and sovereignty, Daniel's faithful devotion to Him, and God's continued hand of favor upon Daniel.

Although this chapter may be the last story we read about Daniel's life, it's not his actual end [spoiler]. God delivered Daniel. Later, He delivered all of Judah. Eventually, He will deliver His entire creation from the effects of sin and death. In the meantime, we can be encouraged by God's faithfulness through the book of Daniel. And in this last adventure recorded about Daniel's life, we can learn what it means to have faith in the face of lions.

Individual Study

Read Daniel 6 in its entirety.

Revisit Daniel 6:1-9

 OBSERVE

What do verses 1-6 tell you about Daniel's reputation in the kingdom?

 UNDERSTAND

What clue does verse 5 give you about the root of Daniel's character?

Why do you think the high officials and satraps had it out for Daniel?

 APPLY

How visible is your faith? Do the people you see most often [those you work with, go to school with, live life with] know you believe in God? How does your integrity compare to Daniel's?

 DEEP DIVE

Read Galatians 5:22-25. **How have you seen the Spirit at work in your life, helping you live in a way that honors God?**

Revisit Daniel 6:5 & 10-11

 OBSERVE

What was Daniel's response to the new decree signed by King Darius [v. 10-11]?

 UNDERSTAND

Revisit verse 5 and zoom in on the last part of verse 10. How do these verses shift or enhance your view of Daniel's response? How do you think Daniel's consistent practice of faith influenced his response?

 APPLY

What are your current faith practices? How would a stronger consistency of those practices allow the Lord to change your daily actions and personal responses?

Revisit Daniel 6:12-24

 OBSERVE

Look at verses 14-15. What was the king's response to the injustice done against Daniel?

 UNDERSTAND

After King Darius exhausted what he could do to save Daniel, where did he turn [verses 14 & 20]?

According to verse 23, what saved Daniel from being harmed by the lions?

 DEEP DIVE

Look up John 3:16. **Daniel trusted in God and was delivered from death. How does our belief in God save us from harm?**

 APPLY

Can you relate to King Darius? When have you tried to "deliver" someone, something, or even yourself by your own strength? What did it take for you to finally turn to God?

What can you learn from Daniel and his faith in God's deliverance?

Revisit Daniel 6:25-28

 OBSERVE

Read Darius' new decree in verses 26-27. How is it different from the proclamation he signed in verses 7?

 UNDERSTAND

What does this new decree tell us about the work of God in King Darius' heart?

Why do you think King Darius decided to proclaim the work of God to the world around him?

 DEEP DIVE

Read Psalm 138:4-5. How does the story of King Darius fulfill this passage?

 APPLY

When have you experienced such a marvelous work of God that you couldn't help but share it with someone else?

How have you been inspired or encouraged after hearing how God worked in someone else's life?

Did you catch this?

Much of this story focuses on King Darius. As the story opens, he is fooled into punishing his favorite high official, Daniel. In his distress, he does everything he can to try and deliver Daniel from what seems like a certain death—but he fails. He resigns to fearfully "hoping" that Daniel's God will deliver him, and to his relief, God does just that!

Yet it wasn't Darius' "hope" that moved God to save Daniel. Rather, Daniel's deliverance from the lion's den was a miracle attributed to something found at the end of verse 23 – TRUST. "...No kind of harm was found on him, because he had trusted in his God."

Throughout the Old Testament, faith [trust or belief] plays a major role in the deliverance and saving of God's people—and today is no different. Because of the saving work of Jesus, if we put our faith in him, we are delivered from death into life [John 3:16].

Respond in Prayer

Our daily devotion to God prepares our hearts and minds to endure hardship. Knowing God's word gives us the confidence and strength to trust that He can and will deliver us. Use the below space to respond in prayer to what you've learned from Daniel 6. Feel free to use the following prompts as a guide:

- Praise God for who He is: Our deliverer, ever-present help, and redeemer.

- Confess any way you may struggle to consistently read His word or spend time in prayer. Confess any area of your life that you fail to trust God with.

- Thank the Lord for what He has done in your life [salvation, daily blessings, and answered prayers].

- Ask God to help you live out your faith this week and to help you live a life worthy of the Gospel in response to the saving work for Christ in your heart.

_____

_____

_____

_____

_____

_____

_____

Respond in Obedience

Are there any specific ways that God is asking you to obey Him this week?
Write those here and ask the Holy Spirit for power to walk in faithfulness.

_____

_____

_____

_____

_____

_____

_____

_____

_____

For Group Discussion

Discussion Goal: Help your group see how Daniel's consistent faith and devotion to God prepared him to face the lions. Help them understand that Daniel's trust in God saved him and, in the same way, our trust in Jesus Christ saves us. Finally, discuss why proclaiming the work of God becomes our natural response to his miracles and how that response plays a part in encouraging those around us.

Ice Breaker: What animal do you find terrifying and why?

Summary of Daniel 6. Have someone read either Daniel 6 or the summary aloud.

Chapter six of Daniel opens with him being promoted to one of three High Officials over the vast kingdom ruled by King Darius. Daniel's track record of integrity distinguishes him from his counterparts, and the king plans to further promote him over the entire kingdom. This leads to several other advisors conspiring against Daniel to see him killed.

Knowing that Daniel was blameless in his overseeing, the advisors devised a plan to convince King Darius to pass a law that would outlaw Daniel's devotion to God. Once the law is passed, the conspiring advisors apprehend Daniel as he persists in devoted prayer to God. Despite the distress and best efforts of the King to excuse Daniel from punishment, Daniel is condemned by the new law to be thrown into the lion's den.

King Darius remains distressed and hopes that the God he's seen Daniel "continuously serve" will save him! Daniel spends the entire night in the Lion's Den while King Darius remains anxiously awake, fasting in anguish. When morning breaks, the king runs down to the lion's den and cries out for Daniel, who is miraculously found unharmed, as God sent an angel to close the mouths of the lions and preserve his life. The king then has the other advisors and their entire families thrown into the lion's den instead, where they are immediately overtaken and killed by the lions. The chapter ends with King Darius' decree to all people, kingdoms, and nations to worship the God of Daniel, who has delivered him from the lion's den.

Discussion Questions

• The story of Daniel and the lion's den is one of the most familiar stories in the Bible. What is something new you learned this week as you studied Daniel chapter 6?

• In the opening verses of Daniel 6, we can see how Daniel's faith and integrity preceded him. How visible is your faith? Do the people you see most often [those you work with, go to school with, live life with] know you believe in God? How does your integrity compare to Daniel's?

• Throughout this chapter, Daniel is called out as being constant in his practice of faith [v. 10, 16 & 20]. What are your current faith practices? How have you seen consistency in practicing your faith affect your daily life? How has it affected your response to hardship or struggle?

• King Darius tried everything in his own power to deliver Daniel before putting his hope in God [v.14-20]. Can you relate to King Darius? When have you tried to "deliver" someone or something by your own strength? What did it take for you to finally turn to God?

• Daniel trusted in God and was delivered from the lion's Den. How has your trust in God delivered you? Besides the miracle of salvation, what are some other miraculous ways God has worked in your life? What has it looked like for you to proclaim the work of God to others?

Life Application

Our faithful devotion to God prepares us to face the lions in our lives. As a group discuss what next steps you need to take to in response to this week's lesson.

_____

_____

_____

_____

_____

Prayer Requests

_____

_____

_____

_____

_____

_____

_____

_____

_____

Notes

**Thank you for spending time
studying God's word with us.**

For more content from Woodside Bible Church,
scan the QR code or visit woodsidebible.org

Made in the USA
Monee, IL
18 December 2023

49960406R00048